BOA
EDITIONS LTD

A SHIVER IN THE LEAVES

A SHIVER IN THE LEAVES

LUTHER HUGHES

FOREWORD BY CARL PHILLIPS

NEW POETS OF AMERICA SERIES, NO.48

BOA Editions, Ltd. ❧ Rochester, NY ❧ 2022

For information about permission to reuse any material from this book, please contact The Permissions Company at www.permissionscompany.com or e-mail permdude@gmail.com.

Publications by BOA Editions, Ltd.—a not-for-profit corporation under section 501 (c) (3) of the United States Internal Revenue Code—are made possible with funds from a variety of sources, including public funds from the Literature Program of the National Endowment for the Arts; the New York State Council on the Arts, a state agency; and the County of Monroe, NY. Private funding sources include the Max and Marian Farash Charitable Foundation; the Mary S. Mulligan Charitable Trust; the Rochester Area Community Foundation; the Ames-Amzalak Memorial Trust in memory of Henry Ames, Semon Amzalak, and Dan Amzalak; the LGBT Fund of Greater Rochester; and contributions from many individuals nationwide. See Colophon on page 88 for special individual acknowledgments.

Cover Design: Daphne Morrissey
Cover Art: *Oh What a Tangled Web We Weave* by Robert Ernst Marx
Interior Design and Composition: Michelle Dashevsky
BOA Logo: Mirko

BOA Editions books are available electronically through BookShare, an online distributor offering Large-Print, Braille, Multimedia Audio Book, and Dyslexic formats, as well as through e-readers that feature text to speech capabilities.

Cataloging-in-Publication Data is available from the Library of Congress.

State of the Arts
NYSCA

BOA Editions, Ltd.
250 North Goodman Street, Suite 306
Rochester, NY 14607
www.boaeditions.org
A. Poulin, Jr., Founder (1938-1996)

NATIONAL
ENDOWMENT
for the ARTS
arts.gov

A SHIVER IN THE LEAVES

CONTENTS

❧

Foreword

Some books are about a given subject; others track that subject, even as they spring from it. Luther Hughes's *A Shiver in the Leaves* is in the latter category, springing from, tracking, enacting many subjects, among them: the conundrum of being young, Black, and queer at this particular moment in time (specifically, this time of increased transparency about police violence toward Black people, this "era" of Trayvon Martin, Eric Garner, George Floyd, of Black Lives Matter); the impulse toward tenderness in the context of violence, and toward violence in the context of tenderness; flight versus falling; depression and suicide versus something like hope, possibility, the belief in. The strength of these poems is in their honesty about these subjects, their ongoing wrestling with them rather than vanquishing them. Hughes understands that conquest is ultimately not an end but a resting-point, from which to prepare for the next onslaught; instead of victory, resilience—if we're lucky, with enough practice—becomes its own victory. Such, ultimately, is the luminous hope that these poems offer.

A governing image across the book is the black bird (as opposed to blackbird), most often the American crow, which in the opening poem ("Tenor") is associated with blackness—not just the color, but the race. The crow becomes itself a conundrum, an instance of blackness that can fly, immediately raising the problem of how to be Black in America is to be routinely thwarted from metaphorical flight, from the opportunity to rise and succeed. Hughes asks:

> Can you imagine
>   being so tied to blackness
>   even your wings
>   cannot help you escape?

And the question helps explain the speaker's state of mind:

> I have wanted
>   nothing
>   to do with blackness
>   or laughter
> or my life.

The association between crows and blackness brings two poets to mind, and puts Hughes squarely in their respective traditions. One is Robert Hayden, who in his poem "A Plague of Starlings" encounters an assortment of starlings (a black bird) that have been shot down on a campus—starlings often being considered nuisance birds, imported here and prone to taking over yards, and in this case, entire campuses. The context, though, for Hayden's poem, is the Fisk campus, Fisk being an all-Black university, in the turbulent beginnings of the Civil Rights Era. This context makes it clear that Hayden has not just starlings but Black people—Black students—in mind:

> Mornings, I pick
> my way past death's
> black droppings:
> on campus lawns
> and streets
> the troublesome
> starlings
> frost-salted lie,
> troublesome still.

Likewise, for Hughes, birds are often a way to interrogate racism. Just as often, though, birds—black ones, specifically—are Hughes's entry point for the existential aspect of Blackness, what it means to *be* Black:

> If not a blackbird, something that was blackened
> by blackness, with an animal understanding...

("As the Fog Rolls In, Night Finds Its Footing")

Here, I find myself linking Hughes to a second tradition, that of Raymond R. Patterson's "Twenty-six Ways of Looking at a Blackman" (as opposed to a Black man), a sort of riposte to Stevens's "Thirteen Ways of Looking at a Blackbird." Patterson replaces Stevens's whiteness-as-default with Black context, not as a way to discuss racism so much as to plumb the depths of what it means to be Black at all, to move through a world that can only see Blackness as other. Section IV of Patterson's could very easily have been the epigraph to Hughes's book:

Always I hope to find
The blackman I know,
Or one who knows him.

A close second might be section XIX:

There is the sorrow of blackmen
Lost in cities. But who can conceive
Of cities lost in a blackman?

Hughes speaks from both these traditions, Hayden and Patterson, and in doing so he argues for race as both subject and context—neither defining nor limiting—and the poems here speak finally to what it means to be alive and Black and a city dweller and a lover and a victim and a son, with a "thirst for tenderness," blackness as eros, as "a forest to be lost in." And always hovering—quite literally—is what the title poem addresses, the ways in which the forest's intimacy has also often been the site of brutality—a shiver in the leaves could be the leaves themselves, could be the birds within them, could be the lynched body that hangs ghostly from the branches that the leaves adorn.

Yet this is a book of hope, of triumph, even as each day that we wake is a triumph over how things might have been otherwise. "Look at all my colors," Hughes says ("Fallen Angel"), reminding us that black contains *all* colors, is in that way its own abundance. That abundance includes the erotic, the familial, relationships variously sought and regretted, relationships with others as much as with ourselves, the self as an ever-restless interior of light and shadow. That abundance includes, as well, the hard-won poems of *A Shiver in the Leaves*, whose music is finally, beautifully, brutally, Hughes's own.

— Carl Phillips

A Shiver in the Leaves

Tenor

After Jean-Michel Basquiat

Crows
      and more crows.
One crow
      with a rat
            hanging
      from its beak.
Another crow
      with its wings
            plucked
      empty.
I wanted
      so much of today
            to be peaceful,
      but the empty crow
untethers
      a feral yearning
            for love
      that is so full
of power,
      of tenderness,
            the words fall
      to their knees
begging for mercy
      like tulips in wind.
I don't wear the crown
      for the times power
            has tainted my body,
      but I can tell
the difference
      between giving up
            and giving in.
If you can't, ask the crow
      that watches me

through the window,
        laughing as I drink
my third bottle of wine.
Ask the sound
        the tree makes
                when the crow
        has grown disgusted
with my whining.
After years of repression,
        I can come clean.
I was a boy
        with a hole
                other boys
        stuffed themselves into.
I have wanted
        nothing
                to do with blackness
        or laughter
or my life.
But, about love,
        who owns the right,
                really? Who owns
        the crow
who loves fresh meat
        or the crow who loves
                the vibration
        of its own throat?
Everything around me
        is black for its own good.
The widow,
        the picture of the boy
                crying on the wall,
        the mirror
with its taunting,
        the crows that belong
                to their scripture.
Can you imagine

being so tied to blackness
            even your wings
cannot help you escape?
About my life,
        every needle,
                a small prayer.
Every pill, a funeral
        hymn.
I wanted the end
        several times
                but thought,
        Who owns this body, really?
God?
        Dirt?
                The silly insects
        that will feast
on my decay?
Is it the boy
        who entered first
                or the boy
        who wanted everything
to last?

Inside the River, I Covet

I have, he says, *never seen lips like yours,*
          and I am serene here fastened by stacks
of CDs refusing the corner, butts squashed
          on the wooden table, ash and ash, a half-eaten
half-brown apple he offers me. And the moon,
          too soon on its last leg, drunk on the smallness
spring breaks, beetles beside us while we watch
          Monica hoop with Quincy in his dorm room on TV,
muted, bumping its head to what we listen to—*Girl you look good*
          why 'ont you back that ass up, you a fine ma'fucka,
why 'ont you back that ass up. The curt smell of cigarette smoke—
          he exhales—soaks the room in a whisper.
The silence splays open, and Monica scores. I ask him
          why he moved to this city, take a swig of the whiskey
I brought in a nameless bottle, nearly a memory of itself.
          To get away from my ex, he shifts in his skin,
he was crazy as hell. I, after promising myself I wouldn't,
          grab his pack of cigarettes, smack smack smack
against my palm. *Here, let me light it for you.*
          The bluebird in his eyes screams, sweetens the nicotine
pirouetting in my lungs as, from outside—*Your neighbor*, I ask—
          he nods—a man yells, *Why am I always the last one on your list?*
Whatever is in the air settles. How will I tell him I came
          to receive his cruelty? Another swallow of whiskey wings
and I look at him: silken, domestic, shirtless—
          Was your ex Black or white? He is calm as he expels,
Black, I only date Black men. I wanted to spoil beneath
          that splinter, that long-tongued thorn.
Is it ill of me to have let lust weed my blood? I have,
          I know, been better, but we monkey into the shower.
How skillful the steam outlines our friction as he forces
          the showerhead up my ass. *You'll be so clean*, he says.
I will, trust, be clean enough for him to whittle inside me—

Clean me, oh Lord—like light from a train threading
its way through the city. Back on the couch, river-dry
    and arrested under *Let me lick you up and down*
'til you say stop, his fingers branch my waist.
    I become his honeyed hanker, his in-too-deep voice,
You like daddy inside you, his spit and purr and butter,
    his snake at the neck of my blackness. My blackness—

The Sound of Hunting

Travyon Martin, Sanford, Florida, 2012

I.

He is screams
and a galaxy of holes.

From habit, more howls.

I imagine the mouth. The blood
crowning, caustic red, the head
of a flattened rose, days sour,
fallen from its stem.

As if there is anything left, I turn up
the volume of his suffering, flinch
as though seeing my fly-flooded figure
pushed in front of the gun's eye.

I am trapped by the anchor of his dying.

The audio is over.

I am heavy.

My hands press against my thighs.

I rewind the audio.

I hear him again slipping away.

II.

When shot once, scream but quietly.

When shot a second time, let loose
the lion from your throatcage.

If shot a third time, transform
the lion into a harp
and strum your way to sleep.

III.

I speak his name when a man gardens into me.

I watch his blood blemish the bedsheets
like a painting gone wrong.

I ask the man, *What makes you different?*
What makes you alive?

&

I claim I am finding myself.

Because I am finding myself, I wake,
drunk in the arms of another.

He is dead, I tell him.

He is always dead.

&

My hands will not release him
into the earth. I give the evening
a loose definition of moving on:
a razor-kissed wrist and a firefinch
flitting the thin air.

The Fever

I came to steal the night. I came
to steal the stars. I came to the bus stop
as a breeze bowing. I came to praise
the ecstasy of sound. Was the road clothed
in the rain's sleek robe? Did the lilies finally
loose themselves? Had the doves settled
their romance with flurry and fire?
Bestow upon me, O wise doves, a sublime
motel bathroom. Bestow upon me your God,
your supreme channel of milk. I can do this labor,
this *O! O! O!*, putting it into my mouth,
taking it back out. I came into this world
as an abused prayer. Bestow upon me the power
and the glory. This night, he gives to me
his seed. And I came into my hunger.
And shouldn't I swallow what's mine?

Descent

In the car outside my mother's apartment,
I watch him ash in the empty bottle of vodka.
May wind, breath hemming my mouth
like a scratched record, the shy swing
of manmade groves fencing the property.

What do you want to do, blunt balancing
on his lips, cat on an alleyway fence.
I shrug and he holds the blunt to my lips
so I can take a pull. *Take your time.*
A car skulks into the parking spot next to ours,

and we shush our lungs. Two children playing
hide-n-seek. But I'm quieter than he is.
His laugh creaks. He pinches my knee.
A scar stitches the middle of his hand.
He settles, and when I kiss him, he shaves

back a smile before asking, *What's the biggest
dick you've ever sucked?* This morning,
the sky swallowed all the day had fashioned,
the bark of the breeched tree he had told me
the name of, which I've forgotten now

watching him take off his navy-blue sweater,
"Got Me?" bold across the front.
There's a dollop of sex in everything.
Tonight is no exception.
You want this dick? I nod. *Tell me*

you want me inside you. There's a bull
in his pupils lowering its horns. I'm eager
to let the Taurus go. To have it cyclone

inside me. He clutches my waist,
and the wind stiffs. I know I want this,

because he tells me so. But here's what I know:
blue jays aren't blue. If you crush its wing
into powder, it will be red. What does
my powder say? It says, *Please stop*.
I am permeable, the fog on the windows.

There Will Be Mourning

Election Night, 2016

I'm taking too long. I'm at a bar ignoring my friend's call. I take another shot, a pill, a drag of a man's cigarette out front. He smacks my ass. *Cue the war on everything*, a white man shrieks. I pray to a god who has no eyesight, drink myself plum for nerves to numb. Someone chucks a glass of tequila into a wall. I go home, cry into my roommate's lap. My mother calls to tell me a woman from church has died. *You know her*, she says. *Knew*, I straighten. Sometimes I react to things I never touched. Behind the dumpster, a man tries to fuck some feeling into me. Blue where it matters. I want my roommate to change the channel. He asks why if nothing will change. The man I poured myself into, I can't stop. Blame "the black" in me. I feed off the recognition. The first step in cleaning is to recognize the infection.

The River

I.

Come home with me,

he says
and then looks at me: I was a firefly
caught in the right nick of darkness,

I—having lost my light, a light
he now seeks, the darkness heavy as a song
or the perseverance of it—follow him.

But there isn't a home. There's an alleyway
and a river we both drink from. First
from each other's mouth. Then, as the river guides us,
saying, *Here is where the animals drink,*

the way heat guides, or, as it is, the way pleasure
orchestrates, we fumble into the fairy tale.

All is how it was wanted: the moon thawing
into a day lily, the music sifting.

Then rain.

Then a decision between receiving the trophy
at the end or the end.

II.

There's a waterfall and river somewhere wonderful
with dead salmon, he says

while taking off his clothes as if they would willow
into flames at any moment.

He is naked
and his reflection scales the river.

It's been a while since I've seen desire
assembled like him. Sometimes, when I sculpt desire

a face, it's my face calling into the night
like a thrush tricked into thinking it's morning.

He walks into the water
and the water serpents behind,

humming: *Come.*
I want to follow.

There, beside our clothes, a rock slowly swallowed
and then released to be swallowed again, mimics our fervor.

Rapture is the water.
We are the rock.

The Dead Are Beautiful Tonight

Even the hemlocks moan.
Black rind, black faces,
winter's stern grip of their necks.

They say it's the worst one yet,
but they've all been the same.
The dead die every year

and I think I'm too good
for such repetition. I've gained
so little this season; the things

I've lost stain the day a rough stillness.
I don't tell him this, but I want my life
to end. He wants another hallelujah

in bed with me and I don't blame him.
Our lives are so ridiculed with pining.
I used to want the romance of hemlocks,

the subtle conversation between
the sky and crows. I can't help but study
things that bare my resemblance

and that makes me a narcissist.
But the crow, headless in the bush,
has been there all week, and if I can't

bring it back to life, what else am I
supposed to do? So much is my want
for everything black around me to live.

Where does *want* get me?
I have my limits, my childish dreams
barreling into the mind's murk.

I want, but I must be careful.
A shower here or a shower there,
the hemlocks will still be a spider's web

of what was. It's true what they say
about the day disrobing into a sudden stroke
of sorrow. I unthread and he arranges me

on the bed how he sees fit, ready to love me
the blackest way he knows how—salt
in my mouth, light in the corners of my eyes.

Leave the Crows Out of It

Half-past morn, the town is on fire.
Sunlight had sloughed its way through

Greentree Apartment Homes, past the sickly
porch lights, the water tower tending attention.

This is my town, my DNA on the eaves,
my flock of goats heckling the fence on 64th,

and him, having known no hills, no 7-Eleven
to mind, claims the town despite the blackberry

reaped from me. My babe-barbed heart.
In the aureus hours of desire, the sky unbuttons

its jeans. We linger into the Eden, the plow
ever-so handsome, plow and heave, plow

and heave, the gawk and hum. Slow
like that. Nobody has ever truly risen

the way my town has, vernal and terribly
livid—bluing air, the blue trust of Priuses,

blue Grocery Outlet inside me.
Arch your back, says the town. I do.

When Struck by Night

For our new apartment, which my mother may never see
since slugging into that old person's disease—I won't bring myself
to say it in writing—I bought a cactus and it's beautiful,
its soldier-green skin and feline-whiskered dress howls
beneath the den light which encourages me to keep my big-boy jeans on.
I know I look for answers everywhere. Everywhere there you are
with your eyes a warless country, a privilege we sometimes share.
But tonight, there isn't a country. Just a sky fussing. Anxious music.
The classic duty of breath as we binge another episode of
What Should I Do When You Want to Die. *Sometimes, you fail*
to love me, I think I say, *the math ain't mathing*—but what could you do?
You've researched plants, I know, to find which could live
without much gusto from its human. You pour yourself
another glass of vodka, a shot of tequila for me. Who am I
to think I'm too good for your anger—you were right…
Come, let's sour our swords together. Come, let morning waltz
into our bedroom all cocky-like as if it landlords the place. Come,
let's plunge forward, drunkenly in love, grab hold the darkness we become.

Making the Bed

He takes the sheets to his nose.
They are fresh out the dryer,
more ashen than any overcast in this city.
When he brings the fitted sheet

to the first corner, his blades flirt.
I desperately want his making to end
with a kiss on my forehead.
But his bullness is what I love,

reappearing as the sheet snaps back
into his hooves. And again, he stretches
the fitted sheet. More puissant,
he becomes fictional. He tucks

the second sheet under the mattress
along the ribs. His arms unzip
a lightning bolt when he whips
the clever ocean across.

What god gave him sovereignty
over ordinary things of my life?
I have endured much this tenure.
I stomached a panther of pills

and was relieved. You know
what else persuades me? Rain
fingering the open window,
my mother's voice singing,

In the morning, we'll be alright.
In the morning, the sun's gonna shine.

I tell him my mother asked
if I was on drugs again.
How does that make you feel?
he exhales, smoothing the blanket

with one swipe of his behemoth arm.
And I think of his breath spidering
my breath, my ass as it ripples
into his pelvis. I am watching him,

my man, and I am wanting us
as we were last night before
we finished and became a moat
of constellations. He fluffs each pillow

as he always does, has.
He checks his work. It was good.

My Mother, My Mother

When I was a child, I would run
through the backyard while my father
yanked dandelions, daisies, thistles, crabgrass,
mowed, rearranged the stones around the porch—
the task of men, though I didn't know.
Blushed with cartoons and chocolate milk
one Saturday, I found a bee working
a dandelion for its treasure the way
only God's creatures can, giving
and giving until all that is left
is the act itself—*And there's faith, too*,
my mother used to say in her magnolia lilt.
It comes as it comes—there's a road to follow.
When I swat the bee away from its fortune,
my father, knee-drenched in manhood, grins,
and his gold tooth glistens a likely tale.
And when the bee stings my ear,
I run to him screaming as my mother
runs outside hearing her only child's voice
peel back the wallpaper. She charms my ear
with kisses. This afternoon, I notice a bee
trapped inside the window as my mother
on the phone tries to still her voice
to say her mother has died. *I wonder if he can
taste the sadness*, the man on TV tells the other.
The bee is so calm. The room enlists
a fresh haunting, and the doorframe distracts.
To believe her when she says—
as the bouquet of yellow roses on the dresser
bows its head and the angles of my clay bloom
with fire—*It'll be okay*, is my duty as son.
My mother sits in the hospital in San Antonio,
motherless—my mother is now a mother
without the longest love she's ever known.

My mother who used to wake up
before the slap of sunrise with my father
to build new rooftops. My mother who wrote,
"I pray you have a great day,"
on stupid notes tucked in my lunchbox.
My mother who told the white woman
in Ross to apologize for bumping into me
as I knocked over a rack of pantyhose.
My mother who cried in Sea-Tac airport
as I walked through customs, yes-ing
the woman who asked, *Is it his first time*
moving from home? My mother who looks
at me with glinted simper when the pastor spouts
"disobedient children." My mother who was told
at a young age she'd never give birth,
barren as she were. My mother, my mother.
What rises inside me, I imagine inside her, although
I've never had a mother leave this earth.
I've never been without love.

Faith Opens the Trapdoor

When I realized the dead sparrow
in the not-yet dandelions beneath the tree
marked depression, not nature's charming riddle,
the sky opening for rain like a famished mouth
so that, at last, the trees could lick themselves clean
of winter, I looked through the tree to find a half-nest
perched at the highest branch. Looking through,

I found not only an almost-home, the branches
macabre, but the question of full versus empty.
I wanted to be full, to marvel at the way
a sparrow fills with the small soft language
of joy, reminding us to survive until next season.
But the tree was sick of the sparrow's labor.

Now empty of wings, the nest proved still.
I believe a thing can be both restless and at rest.
Take the blood the way it's both the stream and a boat.
God is like that. Swelling as he enters
from behind. Sometimes I wear nothing
but his mercy, the myth of flesh. Then, at times,
I alarm like a warning to what's coming.

A Shiver in the Leaves

Are you, are you
Coming to the tree
Where the dead man called out
For his love to flee
Strange things did happen here
No stranger would it be
If we met at midnight
In the hanging tree

— James Newton Howard, "The Hanging Tree"

A muss of flies showers his open mouth
where the blood crusts.

Dead, he will not speak.

I can see how pain chewed the neck.

I rest my head against the tree, sleep
and wake in his call.

Like legs of a spider, his nature extends,
saying,
        Like you I once harbored beauty
saying,
        Like you my beauty takes the kingdom of blackness.

It is dawn in the man's eyes,
a cavern, a slow thaw to memory.

I look
and look
and look.

Who is to say what death is or is not?

He has his limbs, a sky overlooking…

I know he is dead, nothing will change
but still I whisper in his ear,
       Breathe. I want you to breathe.

The Death of a Moth

You know the story before I tell it,
Black and already a hollowed pocket watch,
already thug-boned, nuisance-lipped, white-
woman-smiled. In this one, yes, the cop pulls us over,
you don't have to ask, they were, and yes,
the car's taillight decayed, or we ran the stop sign,
or we were too-Black-too-full magical. In this one,
my friend wears an olive-green sweater and smells
of someone's daddy's cologne masking the after-fume
of Colt 45. In this one, the city sits in the middle
of the furnace's bare chest—it's summer and has been
a haircut too long. The shared cup of water between us is sweating.
Where y'all heading to? the cop asks, dim flashlight caressing
the lip of the cup. *To his place on 107*th. He looks at me.
Were his eyes this copper-glossed in bed earlier?
Cheeks doused with good soil? *You know one of your taillights is out?*
(See, I told you.) *Yeah, my aunt told me to get it fixed,*
you might know her, Officer Shirley? In this one, friend
(can I call you that), the cop knows her—*Oh yeah,*
brown hair, freckles? The cop's hand fidgets.   Friend, when I die,
let it be the body's command. Do you understand? When I die
it will be of nature's swell script. Like how the trees undulate.
Look left, past the cop with lawngreen eyes, crow's feet,
past the elementary school, past the halfway house
I was told was once beautiful and foolish with children,
past the viaduct, and on the main road next to the Chevron
(can you smell the gas), a girl an eyelash short of eighteen
is being held up by a cop for her taillight, leaving a party sober,
asked to "Get out the car," and then as she reaches to unbuckle— —
In that one, don't worry, she is not shot. She makes it home,
throws her keys on the dresser, sits on the bed.
In this one, our cop hems and haws, is leaving—*Be careful.*
The cop drives off and he looks at me again,
eyes muddy now. *Can you do me a favor,* he sprinkles

as he takes my hand. Before I agree, he breathes,
Can you get out and check my taillight?

Culture

The headlights remember boys like us: black, unbroken by the law. As they man us to the curb, one friend says he's been broken before. But not like this. The car parks. Two white men get out. Their blue uniforms adore their muscles. *You boys up to trouble?* I want to kiss the question, make love to the word "boys" as I have seen in porn. We're told to sit. It's cold, my other friend complains. So busy studying the officers' pelvises, I don't notice the flashlights searching our faces, our chests, our legs. I wanted to touch what hung between their thighs. *Got a call about some houses being broken into. Know anything about it?* Prayer would be wise, but I don't remember to pray. One friend says we're heading to his house up the street and tosses his eyes. A flashlight pulls from his shoes to his lips, shimmering. Here, in the Southend, others know this recycled story. One by one, we are searched. Nothing in my friends' pockets, a pen in mine. They don't know how after the frisk the black boy in the porn is scripted to blow the officers. I think tonight will be the night I'm written into the perfect angle. But the production crew never arrives. I'm not headlined. I'm sitting on the bed talking about the rest of our night. One friend says he has an idea and the other looks at me. We know what we came here to do. *Let's stop bullshitting. Take off your clothes.*

In Seattle

Dwone Anderson-Young and Ahmed Said, Seattle, Washington, 2014

I walk through an alleyway of saliva,
soured with smiles. A couple asks me
to take their picture in front of The Gum Wall.

The city carries itself passionately.
So much metal today. So many frames
moving in and out of each other.

I walk. A friend texts [the news].

Ah, they have killed me again.

Art, in its truest form, repeats.

Outside the museum, I static
beneath a man as he hammers.
He is without a face,

but sadness still. A history of this:
men hammering their grief into me,
my grief becoming the rarest wine.

What can I say? I forget all their names.
It was bound to happen.
Everything leaves—

the wet mouth of rain, the throat that threw,
It's never enough to love a thing,
you must do the work, too—

except the trees that, in this city,
become an emerald rush of hands reaching out.
How many times must it be said?

There is [blood] parading the streets, I reply.
The market bricks with whirs and wears
the violent churning of noise on its lips like balm.

I drink a cup of coffee,
sitting on a bench overlooking The Sound.
There is so much blue.

Stay Safe

The dog outside won't stop swallowing the city
with its harping. Sooner or later some good citizen
will peek through their blinds asking themselves
about the fuss, wanting to know what cruel somebody
abandoned such loyalty—some Golden Retriever,
some snip-tailed Rottweiler, who knows. Next to me,
he is asleep, the one I love, the one who promised me
a dog in the long seasons to come. He says when the sun
is at its most weary, when the sky collapses into the Cascades,
when the wounds of autumn vanish into miles of snowy flesh,
then. The truth is, who knows what will happen to either of us.
We are always one bullet away from the graveyard,
a murder of memorial hymns. And if that's the room
we've been born into, why do sparrows break the morning with song?
Why do fir trees fight bark and root for their green?
Sometimes I hear the Earth's sunken voice saying,
Come home, come home. And who am I to argue with the one
who has given us so much? But dear eager Earth, I want him
to live forever. I want the dog outside to have met my dead dog.
I hardly think of him, of how our neighbors shouted at us to shut him up.
One day they did it for us, poured searing water onto his body.
The grass around him became shredded hairs. The flies fevered
and worried. I watched what happened to an animal unwelcomed,
underserved. When I tell him this as he armors himself for the day,
he says that will never happen again. Oh, to be as certain as wind!
Not true, I want to say, but I can't have everything. I can't
have the yellow from the small patch of dandelions, can't have
the echo of laughter rolling over rooftops, over the hush
of engines and bicycle bells, can't bring the dead back to life.
We won't live forever, but I am afraid some wrong citizen
will mistake him for a scar on the neighborhood—they will
take him from me. I settle with a covering spell: *Stay safe.*
He walks out the door and into a spray of sirens.

It Is February

Some odd stream of oak trees
        line the sidewalk like a phrase
that never leaves the mind—
        "I love you" or "I have love for you."

He kissed me this morning
        beneath the gray quilt of late winter
like he loves me, and there's a difference
        in the work of nature today.

Sometimes difference is simple,
        but today there's a woman at the bus stop
screaming, *I hate you you fucking nigger.*
        I watch as sunlight crumbles

against Lake Washington, watch a bird
        that appears, at first, to be a raven,
but with a subtle twitch of its blouse-wing,
        turns crow as it lands next to a puddle of trash.

Is the woman angry or frustrated?
        There's a freckling of pigeons,
tired of the leftover Starbucks. There's a man
        grabbing the ass of another looking at me

as if I were a forest to be lost in.
        There's always a way hunger declares itself.
Is that what it means to be Black in Seattle,
        standing here admiring the rotting moan

of car horns as if nothing were happening?
        The white man next to me looks at me
and shakes his head, mouth shedding a smirk.
        A police car sirens a group of women

not to cross—loud red fowl. If wondering,
         the woman is Black. Does that make a difference?
On my phone, I read a caption that says,
         "Missed two but got four. Next time they won't

be so lucky," referencing four birds, each shot
         in the head or the unseemly breast.
Does knowing the birds are American crows
         make a difference? There's smoke climbing

out the sewer. There's a child laughing
         or crying. In the article beneath, 14-year-old
George Stinney Jr. is killed by electric chair
         for being accused of murdering two white girls.

His Blackness is never mentioned. This matters.
         It matters more than the shot crows,
more than the woman, who by now is so quiet,
         a city of her own. As I get on the bus,

I wonder if she has a son. I want a son,
         which might be weird given I am newly in love,
given that we are Black. Isn't it irresponsible
         to raise a child in this city of mammoth hills

and Mt. Rainier teething away at the sky?
         I think I will die before I get the privilege.
Sometimes I slush through this city
         and feel like I have died already.

Passed Down

To my father

You see him, dead now, you said.
Her and her, dead, too. Your face
so unchanged in the year of rain.
It wasn't the year I loved a man

with a head bald like yours, but after.
Summer, I worked in Puget Sound
and you were happy I was home.
The city told me best: *Your grandfather is dead.*

Since you have the same name, it's safe
to assume part of you is dead, too.
The living room never settled so kindly.
On the walls, pictures of your new children

who later that year refused to buy your pills.
You cried on the phone to me. *Sorry.*
The year of crying. The year of cracking
into men and the men ridding themselves.

I have the same name, too. The year
of collective dying. What I thought was mine
belonged to you first. To think otherwise
was foolish of me. When your father died,

the crows sorrowed the sky and the field lost
its green heart. It was out the blue,
you showing me the old photo, digging it out
from a box beneath the TV. *You look like him,*

a man told me, meaning my grandfather,
meaning already faded, a sapped star.
He clothed me carefully like a tradition,
like a bitter chain passed down through generations.

Forgive me for the meaning I make of this.
You gave me a chain with your father's gold ring.
It broke. I never told you. Forgive me
for being careless with your mourning.

Forgive my bones, my healthy little animals,
for bringing his face into your house. *I'm glad*
my dad got us out of Mississippi, you said, voice
sprouting for the first time after months of surgeries.

I sat, picture in hand, eyeing all the dead smiles
the ground has grown tired of. *The year of extreme*
heat, you said. You opened the backdoor
and the city, being merciful, gifted a breeze.

Aubade

Giovanni Melton, Las Vegas, Nevada, 2017

This is the best time to say it is misleading
to sing in the presence of Death. If you do
not agree, don't. This much is certain:
a father shoots his son for being gay. Silence,
or whatever it calls itself after a bullet passes
through the first layer of husk, must have
stepped into the scene like a musical rest.
Then the scene was just a scene.

It is late. I am in bed. My bedside lamp projects
its numbing. A calmness about the open door
and I forget what defines me. The darkness,
as it sniggers, says to be still. In the morning,
there is nothing but.

He Went Away Without Saying Goodbye

The flux of the intersection was comforting that afternoon.
       The Starbucks was closed. Chase Bank, too. I watched
police cars thicket. Watched the ambulance braid through traffic.
       What could remain of him? Found hideous on both ends,
sopped in his own pulp. Someone from work said,
       Better here than Suicide Bridge over in Aurora.

As I foxed between the pulsing crowd, I ached to find myself
       within the splash, go rolling in it. The spread of him flared
my eyes wide, pretty, while the bust of sirens stabbed,
       and the ill-gotten guts grew ginormous. I was floored
by the thought, the man leaping from the roof like a shirt
       thrown out the window, thrashing its thread and cotton
for the wind. A dance so familiar the breeze would take the cuffs
       and twirl twice before leaving.

During lunch, I went outside into the after-scent.
       The thicket shriveled. Traffic barely combed the streets.
I looked to the sky. It was Pacific blue, blue enough an orca whale
       could swim in its deep. The twinkle of sunbeams serving as waves
crashing on the banks of the mountain range. I was glad.
       Not because death promised arousal. I shook with thirst.
The image painted me hypnotized. But for the man.
       It was a beautiful day to die. To give yourself back to the cycle.

Video: "9/11: The Falling Man"

The skyline adopts him,
        pulls him into its chest
between the altar of smoke
        and blue. As wind coils him,
his limbs unhinge. His white shirt
        makes for wings, molts.
There are screams
        as the man quivers against the building,
is still man. Human, almost elegant
        as flames flex behind.
If I understood his pain,
        I would turn off the video.
Make chamomile tea.
        Within ten seconds, the man vanishes.
I rewind.
        He is falling again.
This time the white shirt wings
        a little longer. I think, *Icarus*,
as the man hurls, fuming
        with each flap. The third time
I watch, I notice details: black boots,
        legs in pirouette, an unbroken window.
The brush of smoke has a face
        flecked with teeth
gnawing the building as floors collapse.
        Before he dies a third time,
I pause the video. I am shaking.
        When the screen dims
to blackness, I see my face—
        whirlpool around the eyes,
famine cheeks, beard of tumbleweed.
        I am dying. I am American
and safely at home
        watching, trying to make sense

of violence. Isn't this, too,
   a type of terror?
When I press play,
   I hear a woman next door cry,
My God! My God!

Obsession Gets on One Knee

Everything is dead. Doesn't everybody see
how the day skulls its dying? The sound of rain peeling
back the sidewalk. I sulk about everything.
My dead dog. The dead deer flashed open on the highway.
A car drips in its passing: *every single day every time I pray I'll be missing you*
Sometimes a tree broken for my misery. Deserted.
A fly hurls itself against my window, each
thump   thump   thump   a heart unraveling.
Nothing…   I am selfish. The birds outside molt for me.
The flowers study new skin. In the mirror, my mouth lurks
behind the dead mouth. Every mouth the same strand.
I give the room its thunder. The fly drops dead.

As the Fog Rolls In, Night Finds Its Footing

What's that story about the blackbird
visiting a man, or, more accurately,
his depression? Making him recognize it,
I mean. It was often like that with birds,
reminding me of my flightlessness.
It was like that, then more so, then only that.

I'm doing as much as I can these days
despite thinking about what ails me—
going on walks, slipping into bathroom stalls
with strange men who become not-so-strange
when they pull down their pants—without wanting more
from absence, if a thing can even be considered absent
not having been there to begin with.

If not a blackbird, something that was blackened
by blackness, with an animal understanding
was in his room. Above. It had wings. No, it didn't.

(Black) Boy, Revisited

You Google "Tamir Rice."
Google says:
    People also ask:
        - Who killed John Crawford?
        - Where was Michael Brown shot in Ferguson, Missouri?
        - When was Jamar Clark shot?
        - Who is Oscar Grant?
        - Who are the officers involved in the Freddie Gray case?

You take a picture of your face. You sleep recklessly. The church prays for your deliverance. You turn the corner like any maggot turns in a graveyard. You're only a matter of time:
        - Who killed Luther Hughes?
        - Where was Luther Hughes shot in Seattle, Washington?
        - When was Luther Hughes shot?
        - Who is Luther Hughes?
        - Who are the officers involved in the Luther Hughes case?

The hole in your head is like any old hole, you tell yourself. A man slides in. Any old hole, you remember. You watch the news, you tweet. Your cell phone dies before you send the picture. You're not like them other niggas you whisper in his ear. You're alive. You're not Tamir or John or Michael or Jamar or Oscar or Freddie. Look how God shows his grace when you breathe, heave when being run through. You count to three before clicking:
    "Tamir Rice Shooting: A breakdown of the events that led to the 12-year-old's death"
A video:
    Tamir…Police car…Policemen…Guns pulled…Altercation…Gun shots…Dead

all heavens are for boys

all will be heaven for boys

boy heaven for all

for all black heaven

will the boy go, will he heaven

will heaven be a boy

boy be black in heaven

all boys that are black will heaven

heaven will be black for all boys

let heaven be in every boy

boys take heaven wherever they go

wherever you go black heaven

heaven goes wherever you heaven

you go to heaven boy

all your boys will heaven

all boys want heaven

all boys black for heaven

for heaven a will for boys

a will for boys is heaven

It's the middle of death season. You live with dead bodies because you keep searching for them. You take turns with yourself, imagine what coffin they'll lay you in. Mahogany, marble. You think love couples with violence. You visit a clinic to get rid of yourself. Before doctors, you had nothing but a history of names. Now you can add yourself, you think. A testament: just this one pill this one time. It's not the end for you. Swear it.

Prayer

After many years away, Seattle is everywhere: the fresh faces
      of the evergreens, the crows that kiss the sky.

I was once the sky. I ran over the hills of my body
      with the son of a man who killed himself.

I've been thinking about what suicide means.
My friend says there are many ways to commit
      without dying. There's joy in that.

I ask myself: *Do you really want to die this far away*
      from your hometown? I don't. Want to die, I mean.
It's too beautiful this summer and I want to see another like it.
The bluebells. The cardinals.

This morning, my mother called again to say she loves me.
I was annoyed, I admit it. I think she is dying
      but doesn't want to say. The last time I saw her
she was limping. She didn't think I'd noticed her face sinking
into her skull. Still beautiful. Blush.

When she hung up, I opened the blinds. I want to die with the city
      pouring onto my deathbed, to the floor, then out
into the hallway, and into another room where it can lay
its head on the pillows of others. Unbound by my bullshit.

Have you ever seen more than one cardinal at once?
I've googled *are cardinals lonely birds?*

I know what you're thinking. Yes, I miss Seattle.
I miss my mother. I miss my father. I never call.

Last night, I dreamt my father and I stayed up all night
          watching his grandson do backbends, cry, and laugh—
long black hair swooped into a bun. My father is alive.
Did you know? Sometimes I talk about him as if he has died.

When the man killed himself, what was he thinking?

When people jumped out the World Trade Center,
          red from the combustion; cardinals; lonely wings—

          never mind. I don't want to go there. I am always trying
to escape too many places at once, flying out of a cage
and into another.

Dearest

Ben Keita, Seattle, Washington, 2017

He was missing, and nobody said to look for his light.
It wasn't asked, but *suicide* was mentioned.
Lynched, first.

It's morning. From my window, I watch a teenage boy
       sitting under a dead tree toss a basketball into the air.

I wonder about the boy from the article, the tree
       he belongs to. I want the dead tree to be Maple.

To be both memory and, like a moon
       hanging in the afternoon sky, here.

It is *hanging*, right? Not *hung*?

I mentioned morning. I haven't forgotten.
Notice how the sky swells into a white flag
       when we're not looking?
How the clouds shackle with weary?

The choice to give up can be difficult. I know.
I once watched a cockroach swim in a sink full of water
       and then with some glimmer of promise, stop
as if the choice was simple.

Someone called that cruelty. Someone saw his face
       and said, *This creature isn't meant to live.*

I have thought myself a creature worthy of Death,
       alone and listening to the city tear the night.

I am worthy, I tell myself. I touch my face
       for a brief moment and the city begs me to live.

There is this breath I take. The meditation of the trees.
Which one is strongest? Which one can carry a boy,
         brag when he becomes a museum?
Maple? Douglas fir? Black cottonwood?

In Seattle, the wind is tender. At times, foul.
It lifts me up against the closest tree
         and the tree, like a bell, rings.

Fallen Angel

After Jean-Michel Basquiat

Blue, what could be sky
unknotted—bluer even
  than a lake shuffling
into the lungs,
and the lungs forgetful
  of self, a blackness
that tars every inch
of inside. Therefore,
  my inside is mysterious.
My wings want to blossom
and ask: *Am I still wings?*
  There are mammals
that can't be named.
A violence. A sex
  without erection.
Eventually, I'm without
closure—transparent.
  Anything can fit:
a heart, a bird, a second penis.
There is a mouth
  I call mine but given
to the wind: red
how blood is red
  when it frees itself
from the *I*. Today,
the *I* is master: a horse
  with wings that pearl
when the blue sky lathers
and the horse emerges
  through the clouds,
the clouds sifting
the faint hairs like waves
  before the horse

collapses against the shore,
tired from being horse,
      howling—the legs howling—
Amputate me.
Yet, I am no horse.
      My eyes sink
into the skull
behind the jelled sphere
      like a snail vanishing
beneath the sand.
Look at all my colors.
      What my body takes.
The sun crystallizing me
into a fossil.

The Wind Did What the Wind Came to Do

You've seen the tired ceremony of felled trees.
You've seen the finches toss their dignity aside
for the hollow mouth at evening's edge,
and the humble Earth saying, *Here, have the night,*
do with it what you please. The perfect moment of love.
Though, this wasn't love. There were bowed trees.
The black clouds galloping across the sky. The wind
moving as if the definition of hunger, going and going
out of habit, nesting as we do when reaching a familiar field,
the natural gust of the body responding to what it finds filling,
resting in the chore of passion. What if this were love,
if wind bargained for beauty, let go of its kingdom?
It must have a thirst for tenderness, stillness in the heart.
Oh surely the distance is closing ever so slightly.
Stay inside me until the storm dies down.

Thine Will Be Done

I came to understand you, dear aperture,
dear sweet sweet apple. I lean into the raven
headboard and place my finger on your pucker.
I tap once, twice, run a line from the delicate fruit
to the testicles' porch, and the mumble
from the backhoe out back digging
into the playground clouds the room.
I came to free myself as Kant claimed,
cuntless as I am; I tap thrice the centerfold,
file my other hand against my nipple.
In this house, we call it *Good-Good,*
Wet-Plum, Bussy-Flower, His.
I want my fill again.
I fish my finger into my mouth
and swim as if a stranger
to the swamp: tongue, teeth, spit, gums—
I'm all there. And where is He?
I imagine He kisses the soft, massages it
into a small pond surrounded by columbine,
meadow sage, windflowers. I dip my finger in.
At first, the windflower winces.
I say, *Breathe*, in His accent of love,
and give myself to thyself.
I think of the night he bested my beast
inside the bathroom after the bedframe
turned tail and the sky barked up its last tree.
I grab the cattail between my legs, stroke,
and sequin my breath with His name.
The sable wishes for more—I place
another finger in. Ah.   Yes. I run
through the field. I hail diamonds
from the depths of my mine.
I moor the hallways with moan
and musk and mire. I want the neighbors

slain prostrate beneath me. Me?
I am that I am what I will always be—
and they? They are what I allow them to be,
a lone lily at the edge of the cliff
begging for rain. And at the cliff's edge,
I come

Mercy

Peeking through the clouds, Mt. Rainier,
with its white tank top, several cities to glare
upon, and a moral blue sky to angle into,
must love by now to be American.
When asked this by the woman in front of us
on the night President Obama was elected,
my mother and I in Walmart—*Isn't it a great night
to be American*—the cashier just nodded,
but my mother yelled, *Yes, it really is, thank God.*
And yes, yes it was, a great night to be American
there between the bags of Lay's and plague
of batteries, to be Black in America, thank God!
But, oh, mountainous beast, who am I to thank now,
years later, walking home from the bus stop,
surrounded by mid-winter-eaten trees and new-rise condos
that my Love wasn't shot by cops at work today
mistaken as someone else? Is there a song for this
strain of mercy? At home, the light flickers above us
as we sip wine, letting the TV wash our bodies
into quiet laughter. I know we should spend this time
spitting on the name of America how we usually do
when another Black person has been killed or when
another country perfumes with our war, but there's beauty
unaccounted for tonight. There are crows out back, tired
from the work of flight and pilgrimage, ashing the branches
one by one. There is the crockpot of red beans in the kitchen,
its chestnut chest bubbling with bay leaves and sausage.
I fear I have made a mess of being an American. Love,
I'm dumb with the fear of never doing enough.
Is there anything else you want to say about what happened today,
I ask him as he takes a spoonful of home into his mouth.
The laugh track on TV peppers the room, and he shakes his head.
What did I expect him—Black like me, American like me,

in love like me—to say after dusting the day along
to get inside this four-walled pasture amid the mourning
of dirty laundry, the painting of a cracked moon guarding
the wooden-black dresser. *Do you like the food*, he asks.
Yes, I do, I say, and I kiss him on the cheek. *Thank you.*

Given

Too slave to mule a word, I relapse
        into him as he into me,

and for brief breaths it was just us,
        bound, stupid stallions laved

in love, twisting into each other
        as he strokes then settles—he is watching

me, holding me there as the sun,
        familiar now of our mythology,

leans into the wicker of trees,
        casting pink and orange and amber,

casting what some have gossiped
        as wonder or a type of wonder

that makes the crows allay their blackness.
        This vein of wonder wanders as a stream

in his eyes when he comes suddenly and not so.
        Dusk is juvenile. He gets up

and silence slides down his back.
        I look out the window.

Winter, Extended

Nothing, just the snow
and a few warblers
released into the quiet.

So easy it must be to be
a sea of white—the firs,
the wreath of apartments.

So peaceful. As daylight seeds
the room, I remember
I want to die. I've said it before,

styled the syntax in my throat.
I'm always sure of the warbler
that finds theory in snow,

and I wouldn't mind that scholarship.
When he gifted me a lick of lilies
in the ice cream shop on our one-year anniversary,

I had not known then how bad
I wanted his lips to be my grave. How dramatic
our love has become. Arguments

I start in our favorite bar, arguments
in front of the storage unit—
I would be lying if I said he's not to be cherished.

Once I realized he left
this world for the realm of absurdity,
I was so caught in the mind's teeth.

It's snowing again,
and his alarm slashes the room.
I'm watching the warbler slip into an essay

—On the Psychoanalysis of My Death

or

—Contributions to a Blue Suicide

or

—Sparing the Mind: The Body's Attempt at Transcendence

You'll Never Love Me

Sometimes I admire the way the scrimmage between crows
for scraps of carrion thrown to the dumpster sounds.
It's not something I often hear these days. There's no shame in that.
Without shame, the ability to foster guilt, am I still considered human?
The drama of thoughts like these breed reasoning. The hue of sex.
I should know better than to sacrifice intelligence for pleasure.
Is that what makes art so desirable? What makes the flesh tasteful?
I should stop listening to animals lose their mind,
but my neighbors can't stop fucking, so why pretend?
A man explodes inside me a few times a month.
He asks if I've ever seen that movie where a group of crows
dive-bomb a boy in the field. *A murder*, I say.
A group of crows is called a murder.

Near Sacrament

Sometimes, it is a dream:
the robin's slick song
paring back the morning—

                          it is not morning,
or, it is not like how morning comes,
as if water from a glass

tipped over, but it is how
I loved you, gradually
and then all at once.

Cherry plum trees
settling into their blush;
hills of sodden wheat;

this golden field
I can't stop returning to:
you, naked, inching towards me,

an adaptation of tenderness
and force—
        brief lights

that fall gently
from your hands.
If only the landscape were that simple:

pollen in the air, each breath
leaving the mouth like a man
pushed from a building—

no, no. He leapt.
To what do I owe your beauty
to which I never fully required,

and yet, while beneath you, is what bloomed.
This is how I began: as dirt
and desire, or simply a small river,

aimless,
but moving—
to where?

Into the City, I Become *Become*

Buildings bastardize the rolling dawn
as the train thunders into the city
away from the home of the man I love.

A construction site ivies into itself.
An almost handsome man opens his book,
spreading the covers until the spine cackles.

Authorities seep through the crowd
in blue droplets as they check passes.
When they ask for his, his mouth surrenders

into a grapevine, and the officer okays.
He *is* handsome, I decide
and pull out my pass to pass the test.

The train is thick today.
The woman behind me chants aloud
in a furlike tone: *The ants pray for strength,*

Lord, for guidance, give us guidance.
Her voice kicks the back of my neck.
The man never stops reading.

They know not because they seek not,
they seek death and the ants are worried.
White with religion, my mother prays

with me every morning before leaving home,
wakes at dawn to lather with *This is the day,*
this is the day that the Lord has made,

that the Lord has made. Light bends
the train and burrows into my palms.
I chant within the dust of my breath,

Yes Lord yes Lord, help her Lord,
help my mother understand,
I don't want to hate her any longer.

The intercom reminds us we're entering
Mount Baker station. From this height,
Franklin High School menaces,

and I bear the morning my mother
dropped me off in front of the school
so I could take my SATs, wetted my ear—

Praying you do well—and waited
until I walked through the school's
wooden teeth before leaving.

There was no train then. No man reading.
There was me and her. My father
had gone off and married his true love.

It's childish of me, but I believe
in true love, in the way it can lumber
the lumbar. How it twangs

the tongue into twinflower.
Too, the yowl of hate.
Look at me. I've fallen to haze

as the train jilts into the tunnel.
The lights flicker, and the man looks up.
Darkness bounces from his eye

to the pole and back into his book.
The world is too silent for hate.
I loathe the woman who baits me

to unleash the spell, drawing in the air
a viscous coat of wasps that cling
to each inhale. The window wipes my face

into some wight. The train stops
and the conductor announces our stay.
Someone groans at the woman still chanting.

The handsome man is looking my way,
book closed, and I carve a smile
for the woman. She reminds me

of my mother, stubborn, never shy
about her God, a woman who didn't want
my boyfriend to break bread with us

on Thanksgiving because *It's wrong*,
who apologized later, kissed me on the cheek,
who was pleased to learn that he, too,

is God-fearing. I know, I know,
but I do love my mother
as does a doe stalking the whiff of food,

gray with knowing what lies there,
hoping it is as it desired.
The woman. The man. The day once dawn.

I am finally what I desired. I take the sun
between breaths, the train's furrow,
the man that loves God with feather and nail,

the mother I was gifted, and throw my head
back into the woman's chant.
My life has been changed.

Such Things Require Tenderness

Into the rain, I walk—
                    the rain falling like light
falls before a storm—
                    and I never look back.

About storms, truly, what did I know?
I knew beauty. The clouds gathering

gray as depression or the taste of it
in my mouth.
                    No, that's not beauty.

Before the storm, a declaration of birds.
Before the birds, a discarded pill,

a black hat with a clipped rose.
I did what storms do: held

against the frail night, made longer
by my wails and crashes,

which, by now, as I dissolve into
the cadence of rain, is only memory.

When the declaration makes use of its boredom,
I'll return to this place to walk again

and again into the rain knowing
I must tackle such turmoil

if, by the laws of nature,
I want to grow.

—The rain is clearing.
I hold out my hand.

❧

Notes

The lyrics in "Inside the River, I Covet," are from "Back the Azz Up" by Juvinelle and "Freak Me" by Silk.

The lyrics in "Making the Bed" are from "In the Morning" by Mary Mary.

The lyrics in the beginning of "A Shiver in the Leaves" are from the third book in Suzanne Collins's *Hunger Games* series, *Mockingjay*. This poem wouldn't exist without "The Yoke" by Frank Bidart.

"The Death of a Moth" borrows its title from "The Death of a Moth" by Virginia Woolf.

The "man" hammering in "In Seattle" is an allusion to the monumental series, *Hammering Man*, by Jonathan Borofsky. This poem wouldn't exist without "In Jerusalem" by Mahmoud Darwish and "The City's Love" by Claude McKay.

"Passed Down" wouldn't exist without "Bird in the House" by Natasha Trethewey.

The lyrics in "Obsession Gets on One Knee" are from "Every Breath You Take" by The Police.

The "story" in "As the Fog Rolls In, Night Finds Its Footing," is alluding to "The Raven" by Edgar Allan Poe.

The second section of "(Black) Boy, Revisited" that starts with "all heavens are for boys,"is after "Everywhere in the World They Hurt Little Black Girls," by Tafisha Edwards.

"Given" borrows its title from the manga and anime, "Given."

"You'll Never Love Me" borrows its title from the lyrics of "Garden (Say It Like Dat)" by SZA.

"Near Sacrament" wouldn't exist without Carl Phillips's book, *The Rest of Love*.

The lyrics in "Into the City, I Become *Become*" are from "This Is the Day" by Joe Pace. The last line of this poem, "My life has been changed" is a nod to "Archaic Torso of Apollo" by Rainer Maria Rilke.

&

Acknowledgments

I am grateful to the following publications that gave early versions of these poems a space:

The Adroit Journal: "You'll Never Love Me";
American Poetry Review: "Given," "Into the City, I Become *Become*";
Dreginald: "A Shiver in the Leaves," "Passed Down," "Prayer";
Foglifter Journal: "Dearest";
Four Way Review: "As the Fog Rolls In, Night Finds Its Footing";
Glass: A Poetry Journal: "There Will Be Mourning";
New England Review: "Culture";
Orion: "Near Sacrament";
The Paris Review Daily: "It Is February";
Poem-a-Day: "My Mother, My Mother," "When Struck by Night";
Poetry: "Leave the Crows Out of It," "Mercy," "Stay Safe," "Tenor," "Thine Will Be Done";
Poetry Northwest: "The Death of a Moth," "Inside the River, I Covet";
The Rumpus: "The Dead Are Beautiful Tonight," "Such Things Require Tenderness," "The Wind Did What the Wind Came to Do";
Southeast Review: "Making the Bed";
Sporklet: "Aubade";
Tinderbox: "He Went Away Without Saying Goodbye" as "He Went Away Without Bidding Farewell";
TriQuarterly: "Fallen Angel";
Up the Staircase Quarterly: "Faith Opens the Trapdoor";
Washington Square Review: "The Fever," "The River";
Winter Tangerine: "In Seattle," "Obsession Gets on One Knee".

"The Sound of Hunting" was published as "Trayvon" in the chapbook, *Touched* (Sibling Rivalry Press, 2018).

I have so much love and gratitude to extend, and if I forget any names, please charge it to my head and not my heart. To the following people, I thank you for your brilliance, guidance, presence, teaching, friendship, and generosity over the years whether directly or indirectly:

Sarina Anderson, Taneum Bambrick, Jericho Brown, Mahogany Browne, CM Burroughs, Joshua Corson, Mayah Daniels, Jermey Edmonson, Camonghne Felix, Lisa Fishman, Aricka Foreman, Derek Holland, Patrycja Humienik, Ashaki Jackson, Donika Kelly, Koach, Keetje Kuipers, Nabila Lovelace, Tariq Luthun, Charleen McClure, Rai McKinley, Jonah Mixon-Webster, Nicholas Nichols, Emily Pittinos, Joy Priest, Gabriel Ramirez, Julian Randall, Justin Phillip Reed, Alison C. Rollins, Nicole Sealey, Danez Smith, Jayson Smith, Monica Sok, Paul Tran, Donavin Whisler, Phillip B. Williams, Emma Ruth Wilson, L. Lamar Wilson, Mimi Wong, Jenny Xie, and Joshua Young.

A special thank you to Eloisa Amezcua for taking the time to edit an early draft of this book. *A Shiver in the Leaves* would not be what it is today without your intelligence.

To my dear friends and partners in crime, Gabrielle Bates and Dujie Tahat—thank you. I have not been the same since we met that one fall evening in Open Books. I appreciate you and keep you close to my heart. Your humor and brilliance are unmatched. To the poets we've interviewed and laughed with and possibly gotten too drunk with on The Poet Salon, your words have changed me. Thank you.

There is much to say about how you taught me at Washington University in St. Louis, Mary Jo Bang, francine j. harris, and Carl Phillips, but I will keep it short. Without you, my poetry and how I read poetry would not have developed for the better. Thank you, truly. To the cohorts in my year, above, and below, thank you for taking time with my work and for your care.

Thank you to my years at Cave Canem and the poets I've met, studied with, played spades with, laughed with, and more.

I am grateful to have gotten support from the Poetry Foundation, The Conversation Literary Festival, and 92Y Poetry Center. Your support has helped these poems exist and fly.

To BOA Editions—endless gratitude for believing in this book. I am happy that in this life, I get to publish with such an amazing press.

To my family, specifically my mom and dad, thank you. I love you.

To my boyfriend: I love you. Let's have a glass of wine later.

About the Author

Luther Hughes is the author of the chapbook *Touched* (Sibling Rivalry Press, 2018). He is the founder of Shade Literary Arts, a literary organization for queer writers of color, and co-hosts The Poet Salon podcast with Gabrielle Bates and Dujie Tahat. Recipient of the Ruth Lilly and Dorothy Sargent Rosenberg Fellowship and 92Y Discovery Poetry Prize, his writing has been published in various magazines, journals, and newspapers. He received his MFA in Poetry from Washington University in St. Louis. Luther was born and raised in Seattle, where he currently lives and works as an arts administrator.

ॐ

BOA Editions, Ltd.
A. Poulin, Jr. New Poets of America Series

No. 1 *Cedarhome*
Poems by Barton Sutter
Foreword by W. D. Snodgrass

No. 2 *Beast Is a Wolf with Brown Fire*
Poems by Barry Wallenstein
Foreword by M. L. Rosenthal

No. 3 *Along the Dark Shore*
Poems by Edward Byrne
Foreword by John Ashbery

No. 4 *Anchor Dragging*
Poems by Anthony Piccione
Foreword by Archibald MacLeish

No. 5 *Eggs in the Lake*
Poems by Daniela Gioseffi
Foreword by John Logan

No. 6 *Moving the House*
Poems by Ingrid Wendt
Foreword by William Stafford

No. 7 *Whomp and Moonshiver*
Poems by Thomas Whitbread
Foreword by Richard Wilbur

No. 8 *Where We Live*
Poems by Peter Makuck
Foreword by Louis Simpson

No. 9 *Rose*
Poems by Li-Young Lee
Foreword by Gerald Stern

No. 10 *Genesis*
Poems by Emanuel di Pasquale
Foreword by X. J. Kennedy

No. 11 *Borders*
Poems by Mary Crow
Foreword by David Ignatow

No. 12 *Awake*
Poems by Dorianne Laux
Foreword by Philip Levine

No. 13 *Hurricane Walk*
Poems by Diann Blakely Shoaf
Foreword by William Matthews

No. 14 *The Philosopher's Club*
Poems by Kim Addonizio
Foreword by Gerald Stern

No. 15 *Bell 8*
Poems by Rick Lyon
Foreword by C. K. Williams

No. 16 *Bruise Theory*
Poems by Natalie Kenvin
Foreword by Carolyn Forché

No. 17 *Shattering Air*
Poems by David Biespiel
Foreword by Stanley Plumly

No. 18 *The Hour Between Dog and Wolf*
Poems by Laure-Anne Bosselaar
Foreword by Charles Simic

No. 19 *News of Home*
Poems by Debra Kang Dean
Foreword by Colette Inez

No. 20 *Meteorology*
Poems by Alpay Ulku
Foreword by Yusef Komunyakaa

No. 21 *The Daughters of Discordia*
Poems by Suzanne Owens
Foreword by Denise Duhamel

No. 22 *Rare Earths*
Poems by Deena Linett
Foreword by Molly Peacock

No. 23 *An Unkindness of Ravens*
Poems by Meg Kearney
Foreword by Donald Hall

No. 24 *Hunting Down the Monk*
Poems by Adrie Kusserow
Foreword by Karen Swenson

No. 25 *Big Back Yard*
Poems by Michael Teig
Foreword by Stephen Dobyns

No. 26 *Elegy with a Glass of Whiskey*
Poems by Crystal Bacon
Foreword by Stephen Dunn

No. 27 *The Eclipses*
Poems by David Woo
Selected by Michael S. Harper

No. 28 *Falling to Earth*
Poems by Tom Hansen
Foreword by Molly Peacock

❧

Colophon

BOA Editions, Ltd., a not-for-profit publisher of poetry and other literary works, fosters readership and appreciation of contemporary literature. By identifying, cultivating, and publishing both new and established poets and selecting authors of unique literary talent, BOA brings high-quality literature to the public.

Support for this effort comes from the sale of its publications, grant funding, and private donations.

❧

*The publication of this book is made possible, in part,
by the special support of the following individuals:*

Anonymous (x2)
Angela Bonazinga & Catherine Lewis
Susan Burke & Bill Leonardi, *in honor of Boo Poulin*
Jennifer Cathy, *in memory of Angelina Guggino*
Chris Dahl, *in memory of Sandy McClatchy*
Bonnie Garner
James Long Hale
Margaret Heminway
Sandi Henschel, *in memory of Anthony Piccione*
Kathleen Holcombe
Nora A. Jones
Keetje & Sarah Kuipers
Jack & Gail Langerak
Paul LeFerriere & Dorrie Parini
Tony Leuzzi & Friends
John & Barbara Lovenheim
Richard Margolis & Sherry Phillips
Frances Marx
Joe McElveney
Boo Poulin
Deborah Ronnen
William Waddell & Linda Rubel